PIANO SOLOS

Sacred Inspirations

ARRANGED *by* PHILLIP KEVEREN

ISBN 0-7935-3550-6

HAL•LEONARD®
CORPORATION
7777 W. BLUEMOUND RD. P.O. BOX 13819 MILWAUKEE, WI 53213

AMAZING GRACE

Words and Music by
JOHN NEWTON

3

Flowing
a tempo

4

Decisively

EL SHADDAI

Words and Music by MICHAEL CARD
and JOHN W. THOMPSON

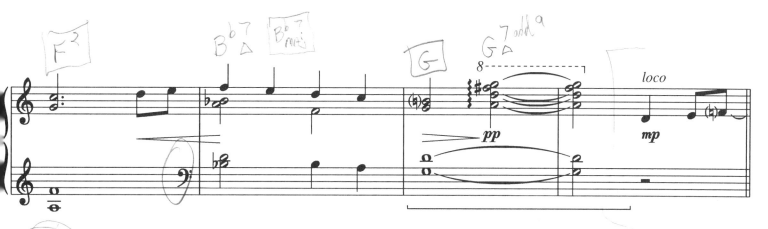

6

FATHER'S EYES

Words and Music by
GARY CHAPMAN

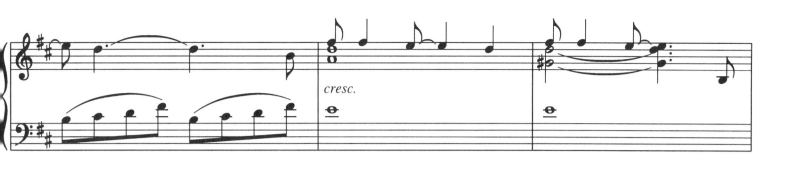

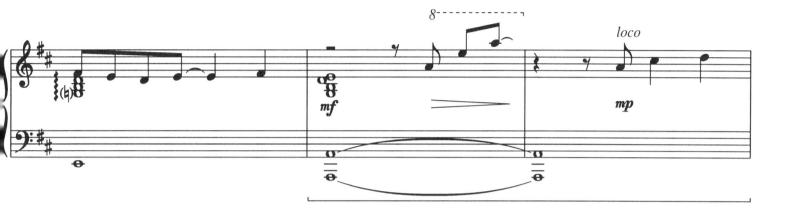

11

FRIENDS

Words and Music by MICHAEL W. SMITH
and DEBORAH D. SMITH

Slowly

GREAT IS THE LORD

Words and Music by MICHAEL W. SMITH
and DEBORAH D. SMITH

16

HOW MAJESTIC IS YOUR NAME

Words and Music by
MICHAEL W. SMITH

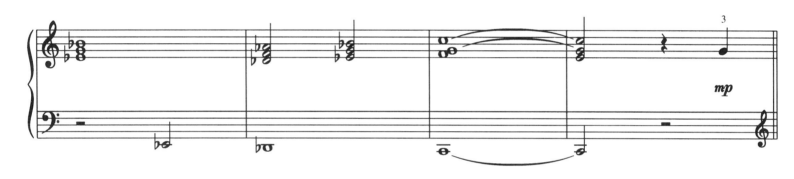

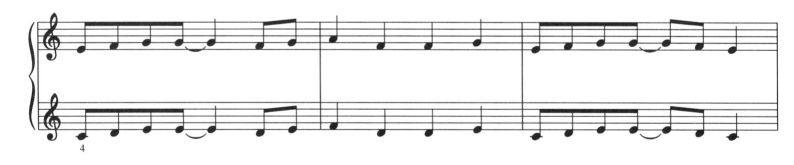

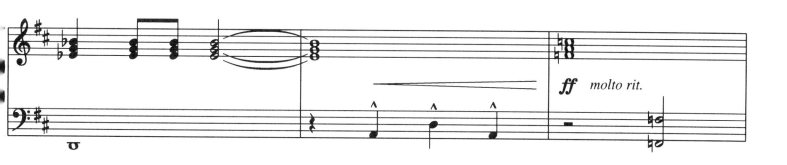
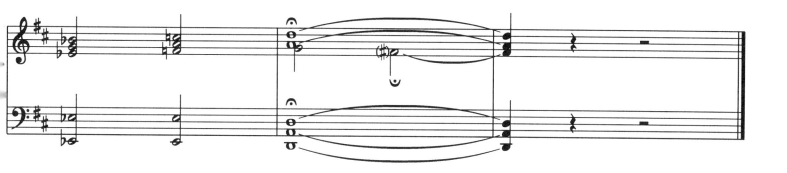

IN THE NAME OF THE LORD

Words and Music by PHILL McHUGH,
GLORIA GAITHER and SANDI PATTI HELVERING

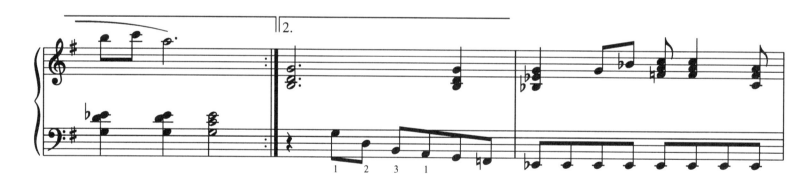

LOVE WILL BE OUR HOME

Words and Music by
STEVEN CURTIS CHAPMAN

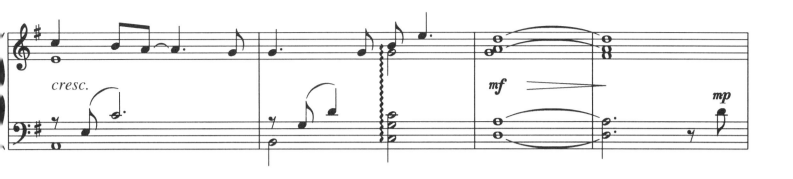

PLACE IN THIS WORLD

Words by WAYNE KIRKPATRICK and AMY GRANT
Music by MICHAEL W. SMITH

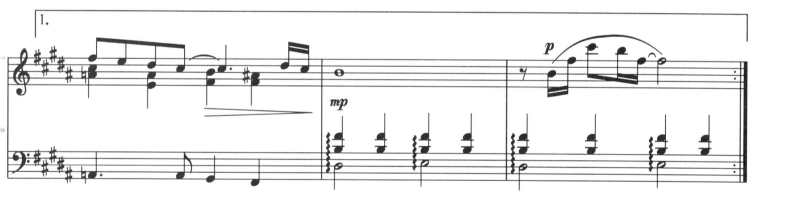

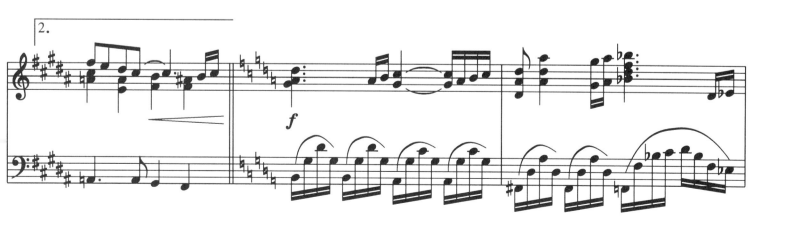

VIA DOLOROSA

Words and Music by BILLY SPRAGUE
and NILES BOROP

WE SHALL BEHOLD HIM

Words and Music by
DOTTIE RAMBO

Prayerfully

(mf)

(f)

broaden

Triumphantly

ff

molto rit.